the culinary kid

A Kids Guide to Becoming a Chef

sarah michaels

contents

1 /
a peek into the kitchen - discovering the world of a chef

IMAGINE WALKING into a kitchen that is buzzing with energy. There's a symphony of sounds - the sizzle of a steak on the grill, the rhythmic chop of a knife against a cutting board, the gentle simmer of a pot of soup on the stove. The air is rich with the aroma of garlic, onions, fresh herbs, and baking bread. This, my young friends, is the world of a chef!

A chef isn't just someone who makes your favorite mac and cheese or flips pancakes better than anyone else. A chef is like a magician who transforms raw ingredients into delicious dishes, a scientist who understands how flavors work together, and an artist who makes every plate a masterpiece to behold.

Chefs are culinary trailblazers. They venture into the unknown, experiment with ingredients, and master techniques from different cuisines around the world.

Their kitchen is their lab, their canvas, their stage. They are the architects of mouthwatering experiences that not only fill our bellies but also touch our hearts and souls.

There are many types of chefs, each wearing a different hat, or should we say, a different toque — that's the tall, pleated hat that chefs often wear. There's the head chef, also known as the executive chef or chef de cuisine, who is like the captain of the ship. They plan menus, manage the kitchen staff, and ensure every dish is up to standard.

Then there's the sous chef, the right-hand man or woman of the head chef. The sous chef steps in whenever the head chef is not around. There are also chefs who specialize in a specific area of the kitchen. For instance, the pastry chef is an expert in creating delectable desserts, while the saucier is a master of sauces.

Chefs work in a variety of places. Many work in restaurants, creating dishes that keep customers coming back for more. Some work in hotels or on cruise ships, ensuring travelers from around the world enjoy top-notch dining experiences. There are also chefs who run their own catering businesses, providing delicious meals for special events like weddings and parties. And let's not forget about personal chefs, who cook customized meals for families or individuals.

The culinary world is a fascinating place, filled with endless possibilities. As a chef, you'll have the opportunity to work with an array of ingredients, from familiar foods like apples and carrots, to exotic ones like dragon fruit and truffles. You'll learn about different cooking techniques, from baking and grilling to sautéing and braising. You'll also discover the rich food traditions of different cultures, from the spicy curries of India to the sushi of Japan, the pasta of Italy, and the tacos of Mexico.

Becoming a chef is not just about learning to cook. It's also about developing a keen sense of taste and a deep appreciation for food. Chefs know that food is more than just fuel for the body. It's a way to bring people together, to celebrate, to comfort, to love. As a chef, you'll have the power to create these special moments with your culinary creations.

The journey to becoming a chef is exciting, but it's also challenging. It requires hard work, dedication, and a burning passion for food. You'll need to be ready to spend hours on your feet, to handle the heat of the kitchen, and to keep calm under pressure. But the rewards are immense. There's the thrill of seeing a dish come together perfectly, the joy of seeing someone's eyes light up as they take a bite, and the satisfaction of knowing you've touched someone's life with your food.

The world of a chef is an adventure that's waiting for you to explore. If you love food and enjoy cooking, if you're curious about different cultures and their cuisines, if you're creative and don't shy away from a challenge, then this journey is for you. So, are you ready to don your toque and step into the kitchen? Your culinary adventure awaits!

Now, let's dig deeper and start our journey into the fascinating world of cooking. Let's uncover the path to becoming a chef, and let's find out what it really takes to step into the shoes, or rather, the kitchen clogs of a professional chef. Roll up your sleeves, young food explorers, as we step into the next chapter of our culinary adventure.

2 /
chefs: the culinary maestros

WE'VE ALREADY ESTABLISHED that being a chef is akin to being an artist, a scientist, and a magician all rolled into one. But what does that really mean in terms of day-to-day tasks and responsibilities? What exactly does a chef do besides weaving magic with food? Let's roll up our sleeves and dive into the details.

First and foremost, a chef is responsible for preparing delicious and nutritious meals. This involves everything from planning menus and deciding what dishes to serve, to actually cooking the food. It's a chef's job to make sure every dish that comes out of the kitchen is up to the restaurant's standards, which means it should taste good, look good, and be safe to eat.

However, there's more to being a chef than just

cooking. Chefs also have to source the best ingredients. This can mean visiting local farmers' markets, fishmongers, or butchers to find the freshest produce, fish, and meats. Chefs need to have a keen eye for quality and also understand seasonality – which ingredients are at their peak at different times of the year.

Chefs also need to manage their kitchen staff. In a restaurant, the kitchen can be a bustling, fast-paced environment, and it's the chef's responsibility to ensure everything runs smoothly. This includes coordinating with the staff, training new team members, and dealing with any issues that may arise.

Another critical aspect of a chef's job is maintaining food safety and hygiene standards. This involves storing food properly, cleaning the kitchen regularly, and ensuring the staff follow health and safety regulations. After all, the last thing anyone wants is a bout of food poisoning!

Now that we have an idea of the general responsibilities of a chef, let's take a closer look at the different types of chefs.

The head chef, also known as the executive chef or chef de cuisine, is like the captain of the ship. They oversee the entire operation, plan menus, manage the kitchen staff, and ensure every dish is up to standard. The head chef is often the one who sets the creative direction of the kitchen, deciding on the overall style and flavors of the dishes served.

The sous chef is the second in command and steps in whenever the head chef is not around. They work closely with the head chef to manage the kitchen staff, plan menus, and execute dishes. Sous chefs often do a lot of the actual cooking, especially in larger restaurants.

There are also chefs who specialize in specific areas of the kitchen. A pastry chef, for instance, is a master of sweets and desserts. They bake cakes, make chocolates, and create all sorts of delightful treats. If you have a sweet tooth, this could be the chef role for you!

A saucier, on the other hand, specializes in making sauces. If you've ever wondered how restaurants make their sauces so delicious and perfectly balanced, it's likely thanks to the saucier. Sauciers are often considered the most skilled chefs in the kitchen due to the precision and expertise required to craft a perfect sauce.

There's also the commis chef, or junior chef, who assists the other chefs and learns the ropes. This is often the first role someone has when they start working in a professional kitchen.

Now, let's consider where chefs work. The first place that probably comes to mind is a restaurant.

While many chefs indeed work in restaurants, from small local eateries to high-end establishments, there are many other places where chefs can showcase their culinary talents.

Chefs also work in hotels, providing room service and catering for events. Some work in the catering industry, cooking for weddings, parties, and other special events. Others work in cafeterias in schools and hospitals, creating meals for students or patients.

Some chefs even become personal chefs, cooking specifically for one individual or family. As a personal chef, you get to know your clients' tastes and preferences and create meals catered to their specific needs and desires.

Some chefs work in test kitchens for food companies or magazines, developing and testing recipes. Others become television chefs, sharing their love of food with a wider audience. The possibilities are endless!

Becoming a chef is like embarking on a fantastic adventure with countless paths to explore. Whether you dream of running your own restaurant, creating delicious desserts as a pastry chef, or cooking for a celebrity as a personal chef, there's a place for you in the culinary world. As you continue this journey, remember: every great chef started at the beginning, just like you. Let's keep exploring together, and who knows where your culinary path will lead? Now, let's move on to the next chapter, where we'll learn about the journey through time and different cultures to understand the evolution of cooking and the culinary arts. The adventure continues!

3 /
a culinary time machine - cooking through the ages

HAVE you ever wondered how the first chocolate chip cookie was made? Or why pizza is shaped like a circle and served in triangular slices? Or who decided that a cake should be sweet while bread should be savory? To answer these questions and more, we're about to embark on a journey through time and across continents to trace the roots of the culinary arts. So, fasten your seatbelts and prepare your taste buds, as our culinary time machine is about to take off!

In the very beginning, our ancestors didn't have much choice when it came to food. They ate whatever they could hunt or gather. This was the time before farming, when people lived as nomads, moving from place to place in search of food. They ate raw fruits and nuts, and meat was cooked simply by throwing it onto a fire. Fancy a sizzling steak right off the flame? Well, that's pretty much how our ancestors dined!

As humans learned to farm and settled down into communities, food and cooking started to evolve. Grains were harvested and ground to make the earliest forms of bread. People discovered that food could be preserved by drying, smoking, or salting it, which meant they could store food for the winter or during famine.

Fast forward a few millennia to Ancient Greece and Rome, where culinary arts truly began to flourish. The Greeks were known for their simple but flavorful dishes, using fresh ingredients like olives, honey, cheese, and fruits. The Romans, meanwhile, loved their feasts and were known for their love of sauces.

Now let's sail east to Ancient China and India, where the cuisine was as diverse as the people. The Chinese started cultivating rice around 5000 BC, and it became a staple food. They also invented soy sauce, tofu, and, believe it or not, the first version of ice cream! In India, the use of spices was elevated to an art form, creating complex, flavorful dishes.

Let's jump to the Middle Ages in Europe, where the food might seem a bit strange to us now. For instance, did you know that cooks would sometimes serve peacock meat dressed in its own feathers to impress guests? But this was also the time when many traditional dishes were born. In Italy, pasta was being made, while in France, the method of making cheese was refined.

The discovery of the New World (America) by Europeans had a significant impact on cooking. Foods like potatoes, tomatoes, corn, and chocolate were introduced to the rest of the world. Can you imagine Italian cooking without tomatoes or Belgian cuisine without chocolate?

Now let's take a giant leap to the 20th century, where the culinary world saw even more diversification and innovation. This was the time when food began to be seen as a form of art and a source of entertainment. Chefs started to gain celebrity status, cookbooks filled bookshelves, and people started exploring cuisines from different parts of the world.

So, there you have it — a quick trip through the ages. Of course, there's so much more to explore and discover. We've only just skimmed the surface. Every country, every culture, and every era has contributed to the rich tapestry of the culinary world, shaping how we cook and eat today.

We've come a long way from the time when our ancestors tossed their catch onto a fire. Today, cooking is a form of self-expression, a way to celebrate our traditions, and a means to bring people together. Understanding the history and evolution of cooking gives us a deeper appreciation of the food we eat and the role of chefs in society.

With this newfound knowledge, we are one step closer to understanding the journey of becoming a chef. As we continue to explore, let's remember that every dish has a story, every recipe has a history, and in every bite, there's a taste of the journey that has led us here. Up next, we'll explore the path to becoming a professional chef. What are the necessary steps and skills needed? Let's turn the page to find out!

4 /
culinary schools and programs - shaping the chefs of tomorrow

AFTER OUR EXCITING TIME TRAVELS, discovering the fascinating history and diversity of the culinary world, you might be wondering how you can join the ranks of those creative culinary artists - the chefs. One of the most important stepping stones on this path is culinary school. But what is culinary school exactly? What do they teach, and how do they prepare you for the thrilling adventure of becoming a chef? Let's dive into the delicious details.

In its essence, a culinary school is a place where aspiring chefs learn the art and science of cooking. Just like a painter needs to learn about colors, textures, and techniques, a chef needs to learn about ingredients, cooking methods, and food presentation. And culinary schools provide just that.

A typical culinary school offers a variety of

programs and courses. These could range from basic cooking techniques, baking and pastry arts, to advanced courses in gastronomy (that's the fancy term for the art or science of good eating). Some schools even offer specialized courses in areas like nutrition, food photography, and restaurant management. There's truly a world of knowledge to feast upon!

The first step in any culinary program is usually learning the basics. These are the building blocks that every chef needs. Students learn about different types of ingredients and how to handle them, the various cooking methods like boiling, grilling, frying, and roasting, and even how to use a chef's most important tools - the kitchen knives.

Next, students typically explore more specific areas of cooking. For example, in a baking and pastry course, you'd learn the precise science behind creating fluffy cakes, flaky pastries, and bread that's just the right amount of chewy. In a gastronomy course, you'd learn how to create a symphony of flavors and textures that will dance on the tongue and delight the senses.

Culinary schools also teach about food safety and hygiene, which is incredibly important. Remember, as a chef, you're responsible for the health and well-being of everyone who eats your food. Knowing how to handle and store ingredients properly, how to keep your workspace clean, and how to prevent cross-contamination is crucial.

Now, you may be thinking, "All this learning sounds great, but when do I get to cook?" Well, don't worry, culinary schools are all about hands-on learning! Sure, there's plenty of theory to learn, but most of your time will be spent in the kitchen, practicing and perfecting your skills. Think of it like a playground, where you get to experiment, make mistakes, learn, and have loads of fun!

Another exciting aspect of culinary school is the opportunity to learn from experienced chefs. These mentors have been in the industry for years, and they have a wealth of knowledge to share. They can provide tips and tricks, share their experiences, and guide you on your culinary journey.

Attending culinary school also provides a fantastic opportunity to meet like-minded individuals. Your classmates will also be passionate about food and cooking, and you can learn a lot from each other. Plus, these connections could prove invaluable when you step into the professional world.

Culinary schools, with their vast offerings, are truly instrumental in shaping the chefs of tomorrow. They provide the knowledge, skills, and experiences that are essential in the culinary world. Whether you dream of becoming a master pastry chef, the next star of a cooking show, or the head chef of a renowned restaurant, culinary school can set you on the right path.

As we continue our journey into the world of cooking and culinary arts, let's remember that becoming a chef is not just about cooking food. It's about understanding food, respecting ingredients, creating experiences, and above all, constantly learning and growing. So, get ready for the next chapter where we'll explore the exciting world of professional kitchens and what it's like to work in one! Turn the page, and let's keep cooking up this adventure together.

5 /
cooking 101 - from ingredients to recipes

NOW THAT YOU have an idea of the culinary world's vast landscape and what culinary school can offer, let's get down to the nitty-gritty of cooking. We're going to explore the fascinating world of ingredients and learn about some basic recipes that every chef should know.

Let's start with ingredients. Think of ingredients as the colors a painter uses. Just as a painter mixes colors to create different hues, a chef combines ingredients to create a symphony of flavors. Some of the most common ingredients you'll work with include fruits and vegetables, meats, grains, dairy products, and herbs and spices.

Fruits and vegetables can be as versatile as they are delicious. They can be eaten raw, cooked, or even turned into drinks. Plus, they add color and nutritional value to your dishes. Think of the refreshing crunch of a bell pepper in a stir-fry or the sweet tanginess of a fresh berry topping on a cheesecake.

Meats come in many forms, from beef and chicken to fish and shellfish. Each type of meat has a unique flavor and texture, and they can be cooked in countless ways. Remember, when handling raw meat, it's crucial to follow safety guidelines to avoid foodborne illnesses.

Grains like rice, wheat, and corn are often used as a base in many dishes. They're filling, versatile, and can be used to make everything from bread and pasta to sushi and tortillas.

Dairy products such as milk, cheese, and yogurt are used in a plethora of recipes. They can make a dish richer, creamier, or add a tangy contrast.

Herbs and spices are like the magic dust in cooking. They can transform a dish from bland to grand with just a sprinkle. Cinnamon can add warmth and sweetness to a dish, while chili can set your taste buds on fire!

Understanding your ingredients is the first step to becoming a chef. Each ingredient has its own characteristics, and learning how to bring out their best is a big part of cooking.

Now let's move on to some basic recipes. Just as a musician needs to know their scales, a chef needs to know a few fundamental recipes. These are classic dishes that you can experiment with and make your own as you get more comfortable in the kitchen.

1. Scrambled Eggs: This is a simple dish that's all about technique. The key to creamy scrambled eggs is cooking them slowly over low heat and constantly stirring.

2. Tomato Sauce: A good tomato sauce is a staple in many cuisines. It can be used in pastas, pizzas, or as a base for other sauces. The basic version requires just tomatoes, onions, garlic, and herbs, but you can add all kinds of veggies or meats.

3. Roast Chicken: Roasting a chicken might seem intimidating, but it's easier than you think. Plus, it's a dish that can be served in a fancy dinner or a casual family meal. The key is to season it well and make sure it doesn't dry out in the oven.

4. Chocolate Chip Cookies: Baking is a delicious science, and a simple chocolate chip cookie recipe can teach you a lot about it. Plus, who can resist a freshly baked cookie?

Learning to cook is a fantastic adventure, one that's full of delicious discoveries and satisfying successes (and a few inevitable mishaps). But remember, just like any other skill, it takes practice. Don't be discouraged if your first few attempts don't turn out perfect. With each dish you cook, you'll learn and improve.

As we move on to the next exciting chapter, let's remember that cooking isn't just about feeding ourselves and others. It's about expressing creativity, spreading joy, and sharing a piece of ourselves. So whether you're whipping up a weeknight dinner or preparing a festive feast, remember to cook with love and joy. After all, that's the secret ingredient in every great dish. Let's turn the page and see what's cooking in the next chapter!

6 /
knife skills, kitchen safety, and hygiene - a chef's best friends

AFTER DABBLING into ingredients and recipes, it's time to touch on some key skills and practices every chef should master. These may not sound as exciting as making a chocolate soufflé, but they're equally, if not more, important. So, let's dive into the world of knife skills, kitchen safety, and hygiene.

Imagine a painter without their brushes or a writer without their pen. Hard, right? Well, that's how a chef would feel without their knives. Knives are a chef's most essential tools, and knowing how to use them effectively and safely is crucial.

First, let's talk about the types of knives. There's a knife for almost every kitchen task. The chef's knife is your go-to for most tasks, like chopping vegetables or slicing meat. The paring knife, smaller in size, is perfect for more delicate tasks like peeling or trimming. A bread knife with a serrated edge is designed to cut through bread without squashing it.

Now, onto knife skills. Holding the knife correctly is vital. You want to grip the handle firmly but comfortably. One basic technique is the "rock chop," where the tip of the knife stays on the cutting board, and the knife rocks back and forth. This technique is excellent for chopping herbs or dicing onions.

And remember, always keep your fingers tucked away from the blade when cutting, creating a claw-like shape with your hand. The last thing you want is a kitchen accident!

This brings us to our next topic, kitchen safety. Apart from knife safety, there are several other practices you need to follow. Always use oven mitts when handling hot pots or trays, keep pan handles turned inward so they don't accidentally get knocked over, and make sure your cooking area is clean and clutter-free to prevent slips or spills.

Fire is another significant aspect of kitchen safety. Never leave a stove unattended when it's on, and be aware of flammable items like paper towels or loose clothing. If a small fire does start in a pan, the best thing to do is cover it with a lid to cut off the oxygen.

Lastly, let's talk about hygiene. As a chef, you're not just making food that's delicious, but also safe to eat. Always wash your hands before and after handling food, especially raw meat, to prevent spreading bacteria. Cutting boards and knives should be washed thoroughly, especially when you're switching from cutting raw meat to other ingredients.

In addition, it's essential to store food correctly. Perishable food items should be refrigerated promptly, and raw meats should be stored separately from other foods to prevent cross-contamination.

Understanding and following kitchen hygiene practices will ensure that your dishes are not only tasty but safe and healthy as well.

And that wraps up our discussion on knife skills, kitchen safety, and hygiene. Remember, being a great chef isn't just about creating mouth-watering dishes. It's also about mastering essential skills, maintaining a safe cooking environment, and ensuring the food we serve is safe to eat.

7 /
the art of cooking - mastering basic techniques

IN THIS CHAPTER, we're going to delve into the heart of cooking, where the magic really happens. We're going to talk about the basic cooking techniques that transform simple ingredients into mouth-watering meals. Excited? I hope so, because this is where your culinary adventure truly begins!

Let's start with sautéing. Ever heard the delightful sizzle of vegetables hitting a hot pan? That's sautéing in action! Sautéing involves cooking food quickly in a small amount of oil or fat over high heat. This technique is excellent for keeping veggies crisp and vibrant or giving a nice brown crust to a piece of meat. Remember to keep the food moving around the pan to prevent it from burning. The term "sauté" is French for "jump," which is precisely what the food should be doing in your pan!

Next up, let's talk about grilling. Grilling imparts a smoky flavor to food and gives it beautiful grill marks. This method involves cooking food on a grill over a direct heat source. You can grill a variety of foods, from vegetables and burgers to steaks and even fruits! The key is to monitor your heat levels and turn your food at the right time to prevent it from burning.

Now, onto roasting. This technique involves cooking food in the oven at a high temperature. Roasting is excellent for large pieces of meat or poultry, but it's also great for vegetables. The high heat helps to caramelize the outside of the food while keeping the inside juicy and tender. Baste your roasting meats with their own juices every once in a while to keep them moist and flavorful.

Baking is another technique that calls upon the oven, but this time for creating sweet and savory pastries, bread, cakes, and more. Baking requires precise measurements and timings, so following the recipe is crucial. It's a world full of sweet possibilities!

Boiling and simmering are two more techniques to add to your culinary toolbox. Boiling involves cooking food in a liquid (usually water) that's been heated to its boiling point. It's commonly used for cooking pasta or making hard-boiled eggs. Simmering, on the other hand, happens at a lower temperature. It's perfect for cooking dishes slowly and gently, like soups and stews.

Last but not least, let's discuss frying. This technique involves cooking food in a lot of oil or fat over high heat. There are two main types: shallow frying (like frying an egg) and deep frying (like making french fries). While delicious, it's essential to use this technique wisely as it adds extra fat to your food.

Learning these cooking techniques might seem a bit overwhelming at first, but don't worry. With practice, they'll become second nature. Plus, remember that cooking is about experimenting and having fun! Try these techniques out, see what works for you, and most importantly, don't be afraid to make mistakes. After all, even the best chefs have had their fair share of cooking mishaps.

Cooking techniques are the tools you use to express your creativity in the kitchen. They're what help you turn simple ingredients into amazing dishes. As we continue on our culinary journey, remember that learning is a step-by-step process.

8 /
tools of the trade - mastering your kitchen gadgets

IT'S time for an exciting new adventure, and this one takes us into the land of kitchen tools. That's right! In this chapter, we're going to discuss different kitchen tools, their uses, and how to take care of them. So, tie your apron and put on your chef's hat. Let's jump into the fascinating world of kitchen gadgets!

Our first stop is with a tool we've already met: the chef's knife. This multipurpose marvel is used for chopping, slicing, dicing, and mincing. To keep it in top shape, it should be sharpened regularly. And always remember, a good chef respects their tools, so don't use it as a can opener or a screwdriver! After use, wash it with warm, soapy water and dry it right away to prevent rusting.

Next, we have the spatula, a versatile tool that can flip pancakes, scrape bowls, or smooth frosting onto a cake. There are different types of spatulas: the flat ones for flipping, the rubber ones for scraping, and the offset ones for spreading. To maintain spatulas, wash them after each use. If you're using a rubber spatula, make sure it can handle the heat if you're using it to stir hot food.

Let's meet the whisk, a tool that's not just for whipping cream or beating eggs. It's great for mixing ingredients evenly and incorporating air into mixtures. To clean a whisk, rinse off any residue immediately after use, then wash it with warm, soapy water.

Now, onto pots and pans. They come in all sizes and are made from different materials like stainless steel, non-stick, or cast iron. Each one has its own special use and care instructions. For instance, cast-iron pans should be seasoned regularly to maintain their non-stick quality, while non-stick pans should never be used with metal utensils that can scratch their surface.

Next up, the grater. It's perfect for shredding cheese, zesting citrus fruits, or grating nutmeg or chocolate. After each use, make sure to clean the grater carefully to remove any leftover food pieces that could stick and dry on the surface.

Can you guess our next tool? It's the cutting board. This workhorse of the kitchen protects your countertops and your knife blades. They can be made from wood, plastic, or bamboo. Cutting boards should be washed thoroughly after each use, and wooden or bamboo boards should be oiled occasionally to prevent them from cracking.

Let's not forget our baking buddies, the measuring cups and spoons. Baking is a science, and these tools make sure we add just the right amount of each ingredient. To keep them at their best, wash them after each use and make sure they're completely dry before you put them away.

Last but not least, the peeler. This handy tool helps you remove the skin from fruits and vegetables. After peeling, rinse it immediately to prevent bits of food from drying on the blade. A quick wash with warm soapy water will keep it ready for the next round.

By now, you might realize that taking care of your tools is just as important as using them. When your tools are in good shape, they'll work better, last longer, and make your time in the kitchen more enjoyable.

9 /
the chef's canvas - creating new recipes and finding your cooking inspiration

READY TO DIVE into another thrilling chapter of our culinary journey? This time, we're exploring how chefs come up with new recipes and how you, too, can ignite your creativity in the kitchen.

Imagine the kitchen as an artist's studio. The stove is your easel, the ingredients your paints, and your plate is the canvas where your delicious artwork comes to life. The best part? There are no rules! You can mix and match flavors, textures, and colors to create a dish that's uniquely yours.

So, how do chefs come up with new recipes? Let's find out.

Inspiration often comes from experimenting with different ingredients. It's like a fun puzzle! How would the sweetness of fresh corn work with the smokiness of paprika? How about pairing the tartness of green apples with the richness of caramel? Mixing and matching different flavors can lead to some tasty discoveries.

Another source of inspiration is seasonal ingredients. Nature has a fantastic way of providing us with ingredients that naturally go well together because they're in season at the same time. Think about the bright flavors of summer with juicy tomatoes, fresh basil, and crisp cucumbers. Or the comforting taste of fall with hearty pumpkins, sweet apples, and warming spices.

Chefs also draw inspiration from their experiences and travels. Trying different cuisines can introduce you to unique flavor combinations and cooking techniques. For example, you might be amazed at how a traditional Italian pesto tastes when made with Japanese shiso leaves instead of basil!

Next, let's talk about fostering your creativity in the kitchen. Like any skill, it takes practice. Start with a recipe you like and begin making small changes. Swap out one spice for another, use a different kind of grain, or add an extra ingredient. Don't be afraid to make mistakes! Sometimes, the most delicious recipes come from unexpected places.

Reading cookbooks and watching cooking shows can also spark your imagination. They're like a treasure trove of ideas, from the simplest family meals to the most extravagant feast. Look at how professional chefs present their dishes. How do they use color, shape, and texture to create a visual feast?

Keeping a cooking journal can also be a great way to nurture your creativity. Jot down the dishes you've tried, what you liked or didn't like about them, and how you might want to tweak them next time. Over time, you'll have your very own recipe book!

Cooking should be a joyous and creative experience. And while it's essential to learn the basics, don't forget to let your imagination run wild. Play with your food! Have fun with flavors and ingredients. After all, the kitchen is your canvas, and you are the artist. The only limit is your imagination.

As we wrap up this chapter, remember that creativity is not something that comes overnight. It grows the more you cook, the more you experiment, and the more you let your curiosity guide you. So go forth, young chefs! May your culinary journey be filled with delicious discoveries and endless inspiration.

10 /
the art of the plate - making dishes look as good as they taste

ARE you ready for another adventure? This time, we're going to journey through the beautiful and creative world of food presentation. Now that you've learned about different cooking techniques, it's time to focus on how to make your delicious creations look appealing, too.

Think about it. Have you ever seen a dish in a restaurant or cookbook that looked so delicious, you couldn't wait to take a bite? That's the power of food presentation! A beautifully presented dish not only looks appetizing but also gives a hint about the time, effort, and creativity that went into preparing it.

First things first, let's understand why food presentation is important. Did you know that we eat with our eyes first? Before we taste a dish, our eyes judge it. An attractively presented plate can make the food taste even better because it creates an expectation of something delicious. Now that we've got that covered, let's talk about some tips and techniques to make your dishes shine.

1. The magic of color: Use ingredients of different colors. A plate with vibrant, contrasting colors is more enticing than a plate with all the same hues. For example, a salad with fresh green lettuce, bright red tomatoes, sunny yellow bell peppers, and shiny purple olives is a feast for the eyes!

2. Playing with shapes and sizes: Cut your ingredients in different shapes and sizes. This can add visual interest to your dish and make it more fun to eat. You could use cookie cutters for fruits or vegetables, or even mold rice or mashed potatoes into exciting shapes.

3. Arrangement is key: Don't just dump everything onto the plate. Arrange the ingredients so they look pleasing. A good rule of thumb is to imagine your plate as a clock and place the main dish at 6 o'clock, the starch (like potatoes or rice) at 2 o'clock, and the vegetables at 10 o'clock.

4. Sauces and garnishes: These can add a splash of color and enhance the overall look of your dish. Drizzle sauce on the plate or around the food for an artistic touch. Garnishes like herbs, edible flowers, or a sprinkle of cheese can add a final flourish.

5. Portion control: A crowded plate can look messy. Allow each element of your dish its own space to shine. This is where portion control comes in. Not only is it better for our health, but it also makes our plates look tidy and appetizing.

6. Cleanliness matters: Lastly, remember to keep your plates clean. Wipe off any spills or smudges before serving your dish. A clean plate highlights your food better.

Remember, food presentation is an art, and like any art, it takes practice. Don't be disheartened if your dishes don't turn out like the pictures in cookbooks right away. The important thing is to have fun while you're at it.

In closing this chapter, remember that the beauty of culinary art is that it's a blend of both flavor and appearance. And you, dear young chefs, are the artists who get to play with tastes, aromas, colors, and shapes. The kitchen is your studio, your ingredients are your paints, and your plate is your canvas.

As you continue your culinary journey, remember to let your creativity fly. Fill your plates with delicious and beautiful dishes that showcase not only your cooking skills but also your artistic flair.

11 /
a taste of the professional kitchen - starting your culinary journey

READY TO DIVE into another delicious chapter of our culinary adventure? This time, we're stepping out of the home kitchen and into the bustling world of professional cooking. How does one begin, you might ask? Well, it all starts with gaining hands-on experience and landing that very first job in the kitchen.

Let's talk about the value of hands-on experience first. You see, cooking is a practical skill. That means you learn it best by doing it. While you've already been practicing in your home kitchen (and making some delicious dishes, no doubt!), getting experience in a professional setting can be a game-changer.

In a restaurant or café, you're part of a team, and there's a rhythm and energy that's quite different from cooking at home. You get to see how different roles work together, from the head chef directing the team to the dishwasher ensuring every plate and utensil is clean and ready.

You'll also have the chance to work with a wider range of ingredients and equipment. Ever wondered what it's like to grill on a commercial stove or bake in a professional oven? This is your chance to find out!

There's also the incredible opportunity to learn from others. In a professional kitchen, you'll work alongside experienced chefs who can share their tips and techniques with you. They might show you how to chop onions faster, make a perfect roux, or even plate a dish so beautifully that it looks like a work of art.

So how can you get this hands-on experience? One of the best ways is to find a starting job in a kitchen. This might be as a kitchen assistant, dishwasher, or even a prep cook. These jobs may seem humble, but don't underestimate them. They can be your stepping stones into the culinary world.

For instance, as a kitchen assistant, you might help with prep work, cleaning, and other tasks. This gives you a chance to observe how the kitchen operates and learn about different cooking techniques and ingredients. Even as a dishwasher, you'll learn how to work efficiently and become an integral part of the kitchen team. Remember, every role in the kitchen is essential for the whole operation to run smoothly.

Finding a starting job in a kitchen might take some

patience and persistence, but don't give up. Reach out to local restaurants, cafes, or bakeries to see if they have any positions open. You might even volunteer at a community kitchen or a food festival. These experiences, though they may not be paid, can give you valuable insights and connections in the culinary world.

Once you've gained some experience, you might move up to more complex roles. Perhaps you'll be in charge of making sauces or baking bread. Eventually, you might even become a sous chef, assisting the head chef in managing the kitchen and creating dishes.

As we wrap up this chapter, remember this: starting small doesn't mean thinking small. Every task, every experience, every dish you create brings you one step closer to becoming a professional chef. The journey may be challenging at times, but it's also exciting and rewarding.

12 /
a smorgasbord of opportunities - exploring culinary careers and the future of food

NOW THAT YOU'VE got a taste of the professional kitchen, it's time to dive a little deeper. In this chapter, we're going to look at the wide variety of roles in the culinary world, peek into the future of the food industry, and explore some of the many career paths you could take. Ready? Let's dig in!

Have you ever wondered how many roles it takes to keep a restaurant running smoothly? It's not just about chefs and waiters. There are many different jobs in the culinary world, and each one plays a crucial part.

Starting in the kitchen, you've got the Executive Chef or Head Chef. They're like the conductor of an orchestra, directing everyone to work together in harmony. They create the menu, manage the staff, and oversee everything that happens in the kitchen.

Under the Head Chef is the Sous Chef. They're like the right hand to the Head Chef, assisting in menu planning, managing kitchen staff, and stepping in whenever needed. Then, there are line cooks who are specialized chefs in charge of preparing specific dishes or working on certain sections of the kitchen, like the grill or sauté station.

But it's not just about the hot kitchen. There's also the Pastry Chef who works magic with sweets, baking everything from crusty bread to delicate pastries and decadent desserts. And don't forget the role of a Sommelier. They're experts in wine and are responsible for pairing the perfect wine with your dish.

Moving out of the kitchen, you've got the Restaurant Manager who ensures everything runs smoothly front-of-house, and the Maître d' who welcomes guests and manages reservations.

Now, let's look towards the future. Food is constantly evolving, and so are the careers around it. There's a growing focus on sustainable cooking and farm-to-table restaurants, where the ingredients come directly from local farms.

Another exciting field is food technology. Imagine creating new types of food, like lab-grown meat or plant-based alternatives that taste just like the real thing. Or what about being a Food Stylist, making dishes look their best for photography or film? There's even the role of a Food Scientist, improving the nutritional value of food, or inventing entirely new flavors!

But maybe you'd rather write about food than cook it. In that case, you could become a Food Critic, visiting restaurants and writing reviews. Or how about a Food Writer or Cookbook Author, sharing recipes and food stories with the world?

Finally, remember that food isn't just about restaurants. You could work in a bakery, a coffee shop, a food truck, a school cafeteria, or even for a catering company. The possibilities are endless!

As this chapter comes to an end, remember that no matter what culinary career you choose, they all share one thing: a love of food. Whether you're cooking, serving, growing, inventing, or writing about food, you're part of a community that brings people together and makes life a little more delicious.

13 /
a pinch of reality - stirring stories from the professional kitchen

UP for another exciting chapter in our culinary adventure? Today, we're going to step into the shoes of professional chefs and peek into their kitchens. You'll get to experience their joys, challenges, and the delightful chaos of their everyday lives. Ready to simmer in these real-life stories? Let's begin!

Our first tale takes us to the bustling kitchen of Chef Jasmine, the Head Chef of a popular city restaurant. One of her favorite parts of the day is the early morning quiet before the kitchen staff arrives. It's a magical moment when she reviews the menu for the day, takes a sip of her coffee, and mentally prepares for the excitement ahead.

· · ·

Once her team arrives, it's a whirlwind of activity. The kitchen hums with energy as pots clatter, knives chop, and the delicious aroma of cooking food fills the air. Chef Jasmine loves this energy, it's like a well-orchestrated dance. Of course, there are challenges too. There could be last-minute changes to a dish, a delivery might arrive late, or a piece of equipment might malfunction. But for Chef Jasmine, overcoming these obstacles is part of the thrill, and it makes the moments of success even sweeter.

Next, let's whisk away to Chef Matteo's bakery. As a Pastry Chef, his day starts while the city is still asleep. There's something special about the quiet of the early morning, he says, with only the sound of the oven humming and the smell of fresh dough rising. One of the best parts of his job? Seeing the joy on customers' faces when they take their first bite of a freshly baked croissant or a decadent chocolate cake. But baking isn't without its challenges. If he's not careful with measurements or oven temperatures, a whole batch could be ruined. Despite these occasional setbacks, Chef Matteo's passion for baking never wavers.

. . .

Our final story is from Chef Anaya, a Private Chef who travels the world cooking for her clients. Her kitchen changes from sleek city apartments to cozy countryside homes, even to luxury yachts! She loves the adventure and the chance to cook with ingredients from different corners of the world. But it's not always glamorous. There are long hours, last-minute menu changes, and the pressure to always create perfect dishes. Still, Chef Anaya wouldn't trade her job for anything. Each new dish is a chance to surprise and delight her clients, and for her, that makes all the hard work worth it.

As you can see, the life of a chef can be both exciting and challenging. It's a career filled with creativity, problem-solving, teamwork, and of course, delicious food. But perhaps the most important ingredient in a chef's life is passion. Passion for food, for learning, and for bringing joy to others through their cooking.

And remember, every chef's journey is unique. Some might fall in love with the buzz of a restaurant kitchen, others might prefer the artistry of baking, and some might enjoy the thrill of cooking in different locations around the world. Your culinary adventure will be uniquely yours, filled with your own stories, challenges, and triumphs.

14 /
the cherry on top - final thoughts and a dash of encouragement

CAN you believe we've come to the final chapter of our delicious journey? We've stirred, sautéed, and sifted our way through the world of professional cooking. Now, as we prepare to close this book, let's marinate in some final thoughts, learn a few more tips, and sprinkle in some stories from renowned chefs who started their journey when they were just like you.

First, a crucial ingredient in your recipe for becoming a chef is curiosity. Continue to taste everything you can, ask questions, and explore the flavors of the world. Remember, every dish you taste is like turning a page in a cookbook. Each bite holds a new lesson, a new idea, and a new story.

Next, don't be afraid of making mistakes in the kitchen. Even the most experienced chefs sometimes overcook a steak or bake a flat soufflé. In fact, it's often through mistakes that we learn the most. Remember Chef Julia Child's advice, "No one is born a great cook, one learns by doing." So, keep practicing, keep trying new recipes, and don't be too hard on yourself when something goes wrong.

Speaking of renowned chefs, let's cook up some inspiration by looking at their early beginnings. Take, for example, Chef Massimo Bottura, one of the world's top chefs. He discovered his love for cooking as a child in Italy, where he would watch his mother and grandmother cook. These early experiences in the kitchen sparked a passion that led him to become one of the most inventive chefs of our time.

Another great story is of Chef Dominique Crenn, the first female chef in the U.S. to receive three Michelin stars. She fell in love with cooking as a young girl in France. Her parents would take her to fine dining restaurants, where she developed a taste for exquisite food and an appreciation for the art of cooking.

These stories remind us that dreams can start at any age, and that it's never too early to pursue your passion. They started their culinary journeys when they were young, just like you. Who knows? One day, it could be your story inspiring future chefs.

Remember, the kitchen is a playground for creativity. Don't be afraid to experiment with flavors, textures, and ingredients. Try cooking a familiar recipe with an unexpected twist. How about adding some chocolate in your chili, or some spice to your sweet cookies? You never know what delicious creations you might discover!

Finally, never forget the most important ingredient in any dish: love. Whether you're cooking a simple meal for your family or a gourmet dish in a professional kitchen, put your heart into it. Love for food and for cooking will bring out the best flavors in your dishes and the brightest smiles on the faces of those who eat them.

Now, before we close this chapter (and this book), let me leave you with one more piece of advice: Believe in yourself and in your culinary dreams. You have the power to create amazing dishes, to bring joy to people through food, and to embark on a thrilling culinary journey. So, roll up your sleeves, tie your apron, and let's get cooking!

appendix: simple recipes to start training to be a chef now

Hello, future chefs! Here's the savory appendix you've probably been waiting for – we're going to cook! Yes, you heard it right. Now that we've explored the world of culinary arts, talked about chefs and their roles, journeyed through the history of cooking, and understood the tools and techniques, it's time we apply what we've learned.

And don't worry if you're new to cooking or have little experience; these recipes are designed to be easy and fun! You'll be able to try them out at home and start your journey to becoming a chef right now.

1. Scrambled Eggs

One of the first things many chefs learn to cook is eggs. It's a basic ingredient, yet there's so much you can do with it! Let's start with scrambled eggs.

Ingredients:
- 4 eggs
- Salt
- Pepper
- Butter
- Optional: shredded cheese

Steps:

- Crack the eggs into a bowl, add a pinch of salt and pepper, and whisk until the yolks and whites are combined.

- Heat a pan over medium-low heat and add a small amount of butter. Let it melt.

- Pour the eggs into the pan. Stir gently with a spatula, pushing the eggs around the pan.

- When the eggs are softly set and slightly runny, remove from heat (they will continue to cook from the residual heat of the pan).

- Optional: Sprinkle some shredded cheese over the top for extra flavor.

2. Fresh Fruit Salad

This recipe will let you practice your knife skills! Plus, it's refreshing, healthy, and you can customize it with your favorite fruits.

Ingredients:

- Assorted fruits (apple, banana, grapes, berries, orange)
- Lemon or lime juice
- Optional: a drizzle of honey

Steps:

- Wash all fruits thoroughly.
- Carefully cut the fruits into bite-sized pieces and place them in a large bowl.
- Sprinkle a little lemon or lime juice to prevent the fruits from browning and to add a zesty flavor.
- Optional: Drizzle a little bit of honey on top for added sweetness.

3. Grilled Cheese Sandwich

Here's a classic that's simple to make, yet delicious. Plus, it's a chance to learn how to work with heat and timing.

Ingredients:

- 2 slices of bread

- Butter
- 2 slices of your favorite cheese

Steps:

- Butter one side of each slice of bread.
- Place one slice, butter-side down, on a pan over medium heat.
- Place the cheese on the bread, then add the second slice of bread, butter-side up.
- Cook until the bottom is golden brown, then carefully flip and cook the other side until it's golden brown and the cheese is melted.

4. Spaghetti Aglio e Olio

Let's try a simple pasta dish that's full of flavor! This will give you a taste of Italian cooking.

Ingredients:

- 200g spaghetti
- 4 cloves of garlic
- Olive oil
- Red pepper flakes
- Salt
- Parsley

Steps:

- Cook the spaghetti according to the package instructions. Remember to salt the water – it should taste like the sea!

- Thinly slice the garlic. Heat olive oil in a pan over medium heat, then add the garlic and a pinch of red pepper flakes. Cook until the garlic is golden.

- Once the pasta is cooked, drain it but save a cup of the pasta water.

- Add the spaghetti to the pan with the garlic and toss to combine. If it's too dry, add a little of the pasta water.

- Sprinkle with chopped parsley and a little more olive oil before serving. Taste and add salt if necessary.

5. Chocolate Chip Cookies

It's not all about savory dishes in the kitchen. Baking is an important part of being a chef, too. Here's a simple cookie recipe to try.

Ingredients:
- 1 cup butter
- 1 cup white sugar
- 1 cup packed brown sugar
- 2 eggs
- 2 teaspoons vanilla extract
- 1 teaspoon baking soda

- 2 teaspoons hot water
- 3 cups all-purpose flour
- 1/2 teaspoon salt
- 2 cups chocolate chips

Steps:

- Preheat your oven to 350 degrees F (175 degrees C).
- Cream together the butter and sugars until smooth in a large bowl. Beat in the eggs one at a time, then stir in the vanilla. Dissolve baking soda in hot water and add to the batter along with salt.
- Stir in flour and chocolate chips.
- Drop large spoonfuls onto ungreased pans.
- Bake for about 10 minutes, or until edges are nicely browned.

You might make a few mistakes along the way, but that's part of learning! Remember, even the best chefs had to start from the beginning. Don't get discouraged if things don't turn out perfect the first time. Practice makes perfect, after all.

With these recipes, you're not just making food - you're building the foundations of your culinary skills. These basic recipes are just the beginning, and as you grow and learn, you'll be able to tackle more complex dishes with confidence.

We've come a long way in our culinary journey, haven't we? By making these recipes, you're officially stepping into the world of culinary arts. So roll up your sleeves, don your apron, and get cooking. The kitchen is your new playground!

Made in United States
Orlando, FL
16 December 2024

55810760R00043